## English Series

# Adjectives and Adverbs

by S. Harold Collins

Book cover design by Kathy Kifer

Published by
**Garlic Press**
100 Hillview Lane #2
Eugene, OR 97401

ISBN 0-931993-35-0
Order Number GP-035

Dear Parents, Teachers, and Students:

The Straight Forward English Series has been designed for parents, teachers and students. The Series is composed of books designed to measure, teach, review, and master specific English skills. The focus of this book is adjectives and adverbs.

## What makes this Series different?

- Various textbook series have been compared. The Straight Forward English Series presents the skills crucial to mastery of adjectives and adverbs as reflected in major English textbooks.

- Adjective and adverb skills are concisely explained, practiced, and tested.

- Mastery can be measured by comparing the Beginning Assessment Test with the Final Assessment Test.

- This Series has more content and no distracting or unrelated pictures or words. The skills are straightforward.

## How to use this book.

- Give the Beginning Assessment Test to gain a starting measure of a student's adjective and adverb skills.

- Progress through each topic. Work the exercises. Exercises can be done in the book or on a separate sheet of paper. Set a standard to move from one topic to the next. If the standard is not met, go back and refocus on that topic.

- Review practice is given for adjectives and for adverbs. Use the Review as a simple measure of skill attainment.

- Give the Final Assessment Test to gain an ending measure of a student's adjective and adverb skills. Compare the skill levels before and after the Final Assessment Test.

# CONTENTS

Beginning Assessment Test ..................................................... 1

**Adjectives** ......................................................................3
   Proper Adjectives .......................................................6
   Articles .......................................................................7
   Demonstrative Adjectives ...........................................8
   Comparative Adjectives .............................................10
   Special Adjectives: Good and Bad .............................12

Review .............................................................................13

**Adverbs** ......................................................................14
   -ly Adverbs ................................................................18
   Comparative Adverbs .................................................19
   Good-Well and Bad-Badly .........................................21

Review .............................................................................23

Final Assessment Test .....................................................24

# Beginning Assessment Test

## Part 1: Adjectives

A. Underline all adjectives.
   1. Twelve people came to this party.
   2. We have few friends in that state.
   3. French, African, and Asian nationalities were present.
   4. Our Persian cat is black and white.
   5. They drove many hours and long distances to get home.

B. Circle the correct adjective in parentheses.
   1. (The , A) two brothers went to (an , a) movie.
   2. (This , These) was (a , an) honest mistake.
   3. How many people bought (this , those) shoes?
   4. (The , An) car went (this , these) way.
   5. The cat left through (a , an) open window (this , those) morning.

C. Comparative adjectives.  Write the missing form for each adjective.

| Adjective | Comparing 2 | Comparing 3 or more |
|---|---|---|
| 1. pretty | prettier | |
| 2. tall | | tallest |
| 3. difficult | more difficult | |
| 4. joyful | | most joyful |
| 5. good | | |
| 6. exciting | | most exciting |
| 7. near | | nearest |
| 8. bad | | |
| 9. small | | |
| 10. active | | |

## Part 2: Adverbs

A. Underline all adverbs.

   1. We always go home.
   2. They have an extremely large house.
   3. We finally found the ball.
   4. She completely built the model.

1

5. They are very popular brothers.
6. They lived there for almost five years.
7. The car moved quickly down the street.

B. Make an adverb from these adjectives.

| 1. slow | 3. gentle | 5. busy |
|---|---|---|
| 2. careful | 4. noisy | 6. careless |

C. Write the correct comparative form of each adverb in parentheses.

1. John studied (hard) of all.
2. We left (late) than yesterday.
3. She answered (quickly) than Albert.
4. Susan worked (carefully) of all.
5. I will arrive (soon) than you.

D. Good-well/bad-badly.  Underline the correct word in parentheses.

1. I wish I could run as (well , good) as you.
2. We lost (bad , badly) at the game.
3. I felt (better , best) today than yesterday.
4. He played his (badest , worst) game ever.
5. Which is the (worse , worst) answer of all?

# Adjectives

An **adjective** is a word that describes a noun or a pronoun.
Adjectives describe in three ways. They tell *what kind* , *how many* , or *which one*.

Adjectives describe nouns, telling *what kind* .
> She wore a <u>yellow</u> coat. *What kind of coat? Yellow.*
> The <u>happy</u> children shouted. *What kind of children? Happy.*

Adjectives describe nouns, telling *how many*.
> <u>Many</u> children attended the show. *How many children? Many.*
> <u>Most</u> people bought lunch. *How many people? Most.*

Adjectives describe nouns, telling *which one* .
> We chose <u>that</u> present. *Which present? That present.*
> It belongs to <u>those</u> boys. *Which boys? Those boys.*

Adjectives, Exercise 1. Complete each sentence with an adjective from the word box. Use all adjectives once.

| What Kind | | How Many | Which One |
|---|---|---|---|
| green | old | three | this |
| huge | cool | several | those |
| blue | playful | many | that |
| delicious | chocolate | two | these |

1. They saw a _____ elephant.  (what kind?)
2. The_____ sisters loved _____ cake.  (how many? what kind?)
3. Ellen gave us_____ packages.  (how many?)
4. The _____ frog swam away.  (what kind?)
5. _____ people picked _____ answers.  (how many? which one?)
6. We watched _____ movie _____ times.  (which one? how many?)
7. Please bring me the _____ drink.  (what kind?)
8. The_____ car was _____ .  (what kind? what kind?)
9. The _____ puppy barked.  (what kind?)
10. The pie was _____ .  (what kind?)

Adjectives, Exercise 2. What does each underlined adjective tell (*what kind, how many, or which one*) ?

1. The big green chair belongs here.
2. That car gets twenty miles per gallon of gas.
3. Both dresses are expensive.
4. This young animal has been sick twice.
5. He is silly.
6. These floors are wet and slippery.
7. The animals had been hungry.
8. Purple and red are my favorite two colors.
9. He gave me that valuable painting.
10. Please include several food cans.

Adjectives, Exercise 3. Write three adjectives to describe each noun. Make sure there is an adjective that tells *what kind* , *how many* , and *which one* for each noun.

1. parents        4. radio         7. nations
2. chair          5. children      8. sweater
3. bear           6. mountain      9. street

Adjectives, Exercise 4. The number in parentheses tells how many adjectives in each sentence. Circle adjectives that describe the underlined noun or pronoun.

1. The soccer players wore red shirts. (2)
2. Each player was from a different town. (2)
3. They were state champions for three years. (2)
4. They are funny to watch. (1)
5. One player will tell a funny joke. (2)
6. I understand why they like that sport. (1)
7. That player lives in a small town which has two names. (3)
8. Practice games are every Tuesday at a community center. (3)
9. The next home game is four long weeks away. (4)
10. That will give us enough time to buy good tickets. (2)

Adjectives, Exercise 5. Underline the adjectives in each sentence. Label each as telling: *what kind* or *how many* , or *which one*.

1. Winter snowfall reaches a depth of six feet.
2. The snowfall is clear, white, and beautiful.
3. The snow lasts until late April or early May.
4. Young plants begin growing when the last snow melts.
5. Those plants which are strong last many months.
6. Some animals will eat the wild plants.

7. Hikers will enjoy the bright colors of the growing plants.
8. By summer, the meadows will be golden with wild flowers.
9. Warm weather will last for only a few months.
10. Those people who like snow will enjoy another winter.

Adjectives, Exercise 6. Replace each underlined adjective with another adjective of your choice.

1. The <u>best</u> answer
2. <u>That</u> one
3. The <u>enormous</u>, blue ball
4. The <u>timid</u> cat
5. <u>Soft</u> music and <u>bright</u> lights
6. <u>Several</u> people
7. <u>Beautiful</u>, small box
8. <u>Most</u> cars
9. <u>Twenty-five</u> dollars
10. <u>Some</u> <u>unfinished</u> jobs

# Adjectives

## Proper Adjectives

**Proper adjectives** are formed from proper nouns.
Proper adjectives are always capitalized.

| **Proper nouns**: | America | Ireland | Canada |
|---|---|---|---|
| **Proper adjectives**: | American | Irish | Canadian |

Proper Adjectives, Exercise 1.  Each sentence has at least one proper adjective. Capitalize it and rewrite it.

1. Who created the american flag?
2. We are having swedish meatballs for dinner.
3. The recipe calls for spanish olives.
4. The alaskan pipeline runs to the sea.
5. Our country is on the north american continent.
6. We are bound on the south by the mexican border.
7. We gather indian corn in the fall.
8. The menu included chinese noodles.
9. The program included polish folk dancing.
10. My favorite breakfast includes french toast.

Proper Adjectives, Exercise 2.  Rewrite the following phrases.  Change the proper nouns to proper adjectives.

1. statues from Rome
2. bacon from Canada
3. pineapples from Hawaii
4. stories from Arabia
5. bread from France
6. juice from Florida
7. pizza from Italy
8. furniture from Scandinavia
9. wool from Scotland
10. folk songs from the South

# Adjectives
## Articles

The words *a* , *an* , and *the* are special adjectives called **articles**.
Articles are used before nouns or before other adjectives describing nouns.

Use the indefinite *a* before words that begin with a consonant sound.

    a car       a large car       a sweater       a red sweater

Use the indefinite *an* before words beginning with a vowel sound or silent *h* .

    an elephant       an open window       an hour

Use *the* before singular or plural words indicating a particular place or thing.

    the animal       the open window       the sweater

Articles, Exercise 1.  Circle the correct adjective.  Underline the noun it describes.

1. (The  ,  A) two brothers went to (a  ,  an) movie.
2. Can you wash (the  ,  a) plates?
3. (An  ,  A) unusual cat ran to the door.
4. I received a card from (a  ,  an) old uncle in Virginia.
5. We will go home after (the  ,  an) play.
6. Let's take (the  ,  an) picture home.
7. We took (a  ,  an) walk across town.
8. How far away is (the  ,  a) school you attend?
9. We took (a  ,  an) boat to (a  ,  an) island.
10. He ran around (the  ,  an) track twice.

Articles, Exercise 2.  Circle the correct adjective in each sentence.

1. (A  ,  An) hot pan burned the table top.
2. It had been (the  ,  a) hard decision to make.
3. (A  ,  An) happy person makes other people happy, too.
4. His present was (a  ,  an) enormous box of candy.
5. She received (a  ,  an) beautiful orchid.
6. (The  ,  A) beautiful clothes were expensive.
7. It was (a  ,  an) honest mistake.
8. We took (a  ,  an) motor boat to (a  ,  an) deserted island.
9. (The  ,  A) open window was on (the  ,  an) second floor.
10. Some say that he was (a  ,  an) great actor.

# Adjectives
## Demonstrative Adjectives

The words *this* , *that* , *these* , and *those*  are special adjectives called **demonstrative adjectives**. Demonstrative adjectives are used to point out something.

*This* and *that* describe singular nouns.
*These* and *those* describe plural nouns.

*This* and *these* refer to people and things that are close.
> This boy is tall.        Look at these people.

*That* and *those* refer to people and things that are far away.
> That building is far away.      Those stars are lovely.

**Be careful**. *This* , *that* , *these* , and *those*  can be used as pronouns. When any of these four words do not describe other words in a sentence, they are pronouns.

> That is yours.        Who said that?        These are mine.

Demonstrative Adjectives, Exercise 1.  Circle the correct demonstrative adjective. Underline the noun it describes.

1. (This  ,  These) book is about famous inventors.
2. How many people bought (this  ,  those) shoes?
3. (That  ,  Those) doctor is very polite.
4. Please hand me (that  ,  those)  papers.
5. They were not going to (that  ,  those) house.
6. Take (these  ,  this) books home with you.
7. Take (that  ,  these) box of wood.
8. (This  ,  Those) old stories are enjoyable.
9. (That  ,  These) green glass has a crack.
10. Many strange insects are found in (that, these) Western states.

Demonstrative Adjectives, Exercise 2. Label the **bold** word as a pronoun or adjective.

1. **This** hat belongs to me.
2. **That** is my hat.
3. **These** books are for you.
4. **These** are for you and your brother.
5. **Those** go with the shirt.
6. **This** is your coat.
7. She took **those** with her.
8. **Those** shirts must be washed.
9. His cat is **this** one.
10. Give **these** to him.
11. What is **this**?
12. **These** are greener.
13. **That** was fast.
14. **This** cake is mine.
15. **That** cake is yours.

# Adjectives

## Comparative Adjectives

Adjectives have special forms to **compare** two or more nouns.

Add *-er* or *more* to compare two nouns.
Add *-est* or *most* to compare more than two nouns.

Usually *-er* or *-est* is added to one-syllable adjectives. Most adjectives with two or more syllables use *more* or *most* before the adjective.

| Adjectives | Comparing two (comparative form) | Comparing three or more (superlative form) |
|---|---|---|
| **One Syllable** | | |
| big | bigger | biggest |
| strong | stronger | strongest |
| | | |
| **Two or more Syllables** | | |
| careful | more careful | most careful |
| important | more important | most important |

Comparative Adjectives, Exercise 1. Add the missing form for each word.

| Adjective | Two | Three or More |
|---|---|---|
| fast | | fastest |
| tall | taller | |
| popular | | most popular |
| | heavier | |
| | more famous | most famous |
| green | | greenest |
| messy | | messiest |
| expensive | more expensive | |
| wet | wetter | |
| | more difficult | |
| pretty | | |
| powerful | | |
| exciting | | |
| beautiful | | |
| active | | |
| small | | |
| young | | |

| Adjective | Two | Three or More |
|-----------|-----|---------------|
| successful | | |
| hot | | |
| new | | |
| wise | | |
| comfortable | | |
| happy | | |
| clever | | |
| heavy | | |

Comparative Adjectives, Exercise 2. Use the comparative form of the adjective in parentheses.

1. Which of the three is the _____ . (deep)
2. Elena is the _____ player of all. (fast)
3. She tells the _____ jokes I have ever heard. (funny)
4. This book is _____ than that one. (difficult)
5. My ring is _____ than yours. (pretty)
6. Janet told me the _____ story of all. (surprising)
7. This is the _____ I have ever been. (comfortable)
8. He is the _____ person you could meet. (nice)
9. Mexico is the _____ country of the two. (warm)
10. Kansas is _____ than Oregon. (flat)

Comparative Adjectives, Exercise 3. Underline the correct comparative adjective.

1. The three (more , most) expensive coats were made of wool.
2. He is (heavier , more heavy) than last year.
3. Those are the (greenest , greener) flowers I have ever seen.
4. Which pole is (longest , more long)?
5. It is (harder , hardest) to run than walk.
6. Mary carves the (most beautiful , beautifulest) wooden figures.
7. Can you find a (comfortabler , more comfortable) seat?
8. They choose the (freshest , more fresh) apples.
9. My wife is a (fancier , more fancy) cook than I am.
10. This box is (light , lighter).

# Adjectives

## Special Adjectives

The adjectives *good* and *bad* have special comparative forms.

| Adjective | Comparing 2 nouns/pronouns | Comparing 3 or more nouns/pronouns |
|-----------|----------------------------|-------------------------------------|
| good | better | best |
| bad | worse | worst |

Do not use *more* or *most* with these two special adjectives.

Good and Bad, Exercise 1. Underline the correct word in each sentence.

1. You do your (good , best) work in math.
2. My cold is (worse , worst) today than it was yesterday.
3. The (better , best) answer of all was yours.
4. His was a (good , better) answer, but yours was (better , best).
5. That was the (worse , worst) of all possibilities.
6. You did a (good , better) job than anyone else.
7. My sister is the (better , best) cook in our family.
8. I am the (worse , worst) cook in our family.
9. I am a (better , best) writer today than last year.
10. I thought I was (bad , worse), but you are (worse , worst).

Good and Bad, Exercise 2. Write the correct form of the word in the parentheses.

1. John is _____ at golf. (bad)
2. He is much _____ at volleyball than golf. (good)
3. His sister is the _____ golfer in the nation. (good)
4. She is also the _____ of all swimmers. (bad)
5. Susan wants to be a _____ swimmer than she is now. (good)
6. You made a _____ choice today. (good)
7. It was the _____ of all possibilities. (good)
8. We received the _____ news of all today. (bad)
9. Your idea is _____ than his. (bad).
10. Given two choices, which is _____ ? (good)

# **R**eview

A. Circle all proper adjectives. Underline all other adjectives that tell *what kind* , *how many* , or *which one* .

1. How many people live in the green building?
2. The apple pie was warm and tasty.
3. They are Washington apples.
4. Our Persian cat is old, but she is beautiful.
5. Wood stoves should burn dry wood.
6. Those tin cans came from the corner market.
7. Some people will bring large boxes.
8. The entire school will attend the free concert.
9. Today is a perfect day to repair the broken door.
10. The last train left ten minutes ago.

B. Underline the correct article or demonstrative adjective.

1. (This  , Those) dog is (a  , an) golden retriever.
2. (A  , An) history test will be given on Friday.
3. Would you rather have a cherry or (a  ,  an) olive?
4. (These  , That) book belongs on the top shelf.
5. The work will take (a  ,  an) hour to complete.

C. Use the correct form of the adjective in parentheses.

1. My mother makes the_____ cookies in the world.  (good)
2. This is the_____ storm this year.  (bad)
3. What is the_____ day of the year?  (long)
4. Is this one or that one_____ ?  (beautiful)
5. The_____ part of all is remembering to come on time.  (hard)
6. That is the_____ recipe of the two.  (good)
7. The oak has_____ and _____ wood than the pine.  (strong)  (heavy)
8. Your answer is_____ than his.  (bad)
9. Which of you two has studied _____ ?  (long)
10. Who is the _____ student in your class?  (successful)

# Adverbs

An adverb describes a verb, an adjective, or another adverb.

**Adverbs Describing Verbs.**

Adverbs tell *how* : John writes *well* .

Well tells how John *writes* .

Adverbs tell *when* : We *often* go fishing.

*Often* tells when we *go* .

Adverbs tell *where* : Sara lives *nearby* .

*Nearby* tells where Sara *lives* .

Examples of some adverbs that might be used to describe verbs:
How: quickly, alone, proudly, easily
When: now, later, often, soon, immediately
Where: here, below, nearby, up, away

Adverbs can take different positions in sentences:
**Before verbs:** Relatives often come to visit.
**After verbs:** Relatives come often to visit.
**At the beginning:** Often, relatives come to visit.
**At the end:** Relatives come to visit often.

Adverbs and Verbs, Exercise 1. The verbs are underlined. Write the adverb which describes each verb. A hint is given.

1. He <u>moved</u> carefully. (how)
2. Alice <u>ran</u> to the car quietly. (how)
3. The sun <u>is</u> now <u>setting</u>. (when)
4. What time <u>will</u> they <u>come</u> here? (where)
5. Our mail <u>arrived</u> yesterday. (when)

Adverbs and Verbs, Exercise 2. Read each sentence. Underline each adverb that could complete the sentence.

1. My father looked _____ for his shoes.

    everywhere_____ quick        carefully        nice

2. _____ the whistle blew.

    Instantly        Loud        Suddenly        Sharp

3. We _____ eat with our grandparents.
      often       happily     now        sometimes
4. The parade began _____ .
      early       quick     noisily        white
5. The music will begin _____ .
      soon       cheerful    shortly    loudly

Adverbs and Verbs, Exercise 3. The adverb is underlined in each sentence. Write whether it tells *how* , *when* , or *where* .

1. The dog ate <u>hungrily</u>.
2. I will finish my book <u>tonight</u>.
3. Leaves were scattered <u>everywhere</u>.
4. She <u>easily</u> won the final race.
5. <u>Nearby</u> the crowds cheered.
6. Robert awoke <u>early</u> on Sunday.
7. He walked <u>carefully</u> on the wet floor.
8. Your answer will come <u>soon</u>.
9. They walked <u>quietly</u> along the gravel path.
10. The balloons floated <u>overhead</u>.

Adverbs and Verbs, Exercise 4. Underline the verb with its adverb for each sentence. Then, write whether the adverb tells *how* , *when* , or *where* .

1. The hikers walked slowly.
2. The white paint dried overnight.
3. She stood above the crowd.
4. He won the prize fairly.
5. The firewood was placed inside.
6. We opened our presents excitedly.
7. Happily we watched the show on television.
8. Please give me an answer sometime.
9. She can jump easily over the obstacle.
10. Today he brought the newspaper.

Adverbs and Verbs, Exercise 5. Which adverb will best complete the sentence? Use each adverb only once.

| How: | badly | politely | tremendously |
|---|---|---|---|
| When: | early | suddenly | later |
| Where: | there | outside | everywhere |

1. You left your coat (where).
2. Was he (how) hurt?
3. She (how) introduced me to the president.

4. We arrived (when) to meet the plane.
5. They had been shopping (where) in town.
6. The earthquake came (when) last night.
7. Scott returned (when) to get his coat.
8. The crowd moved (where) into the street.
9. He helped us (how).

## Adverbs Describing Adjectives.

An adverb can explain more about an adjective. Adverbs that describe adjectives usually tell *how* (to what extent) or *how often*.

Sara is a <u>very</u> popular student.  *Very* tells how popular.

The river is <u>extremely</u> wide.  *Extremely* tells how wide.

Adverbs often used to describe adjectives are:

| | |
|---|---|
| very | really |
| too | hardly |
| extremely | quite |

Adverbs and Adjectives, Exercise 1.  The adjectives are underlined.  Write the adverb which describes each underlined adjective.

1. The house was awfully <u>small</u>.
2. She became a very <u>popular</u> teacher.
3. My father was quite <u>happy</u> with us.
4. September is a really <u>beautiful</u> month.
5. Often he is <u>nice</u>.  (when)
6. They live in an extremely <u>large</u> house.
7. The story was unusually <u>short</u>.
8. Many very <u>important</u> people came.
9. I have lived here nearly <u>five</u> years.
10. My sister has a very <u>big</u> bedroom.

Adverbs and Adjectives, Exercise 2.  Choose an adverb to describe the underlined adjective and write it in the blank.  Do not use an adverb more than once.

1. The animals seem _____ <u>happy</u>.
2. That music is_____ <u>soothing</u>.
3. The_____ <u>full</u> cup was tipped over.
4. The river became _____ <u>narrow</u>.
5. The view of the valley was_____ <u>lovely</u>.

**Adverbs Describing Adverbs.**

Adverbs can modify other adverbs. When they do, they strengthen the meaning of the adverb they modify.

Use adverbs sparingly to modify other adverbs.

Commonly used modifying adverbs are: really, very, too, quite, rather.

Adverbs and Adverbs, Exercise 1. An adverb is underlined in each sentence. Circle the other adverb that modifies it.

1. The crowd was very quiet.
2. He placed them closely together.
3. The train left quite quickly.
4. People too often forget.
5. The trip was really carefully planned.
6. They talked so slowly.
7. John writes very well.
8. The calf was too sickly.
9. The people shouted rather loudly.
10. The cat jumped somewhat eagerly.

# Adverbs

## -ly Adverbs

Some adverbs are formed by adding *-ly* to adjectives.

Most adverbs formed from adjectives tell how an action happened. Here are some spelling changes to remember when changing adjectives to adverbs.

| Adjective + ly | Adverb | Spelling Changes |
| --- | --- | --- |
| 1. rare + ly | rarely | -vcv ending, add -ly |
| 2. careful + ly | carefully | -cvc ending, add -ly |
|    slow + ly | slowly | |
| 3. cost + ly | costly | -vcc ending, add -ly |
| 4. gentle + ly | gently | -ccv ending, drop the final cv, add -ly |
| 5. cosy + ly | cosily | -y ending, -y is changed to -i, add -ly |

-ly, Exercise 1. Change the following adjectives to adverbs. Make the necessary spelling changes.

| | | | |
| --- | --- | --- | --- |
| 1. quiet | 6. angry | 11. playful | 16. easy |
| 2. quick | 7. truthful | 12. dear | 17. careless |
| 3. sudden | 8. happy | 13. simple | 18. noisy |
| 4. close | 9. usual | 14. selfish | 19. tender |
| 5. sure | 10. lazy | 15. sleepy | 20. busy |

-ly, Exercise 2. Change each adjective in the parentheses to an adverb.

1. She finished her work (immediate).
2. He speaks so (soft) that you must listen (close).
3. They (bare) escaped the storm.
4. The children missed each other (terrible).
5. Could you (possible) be wrong?
6. It is (extreme) important that you answer (quick).
7. That story (real) happened.
8. (Sad), this is (exact) what happened.
9. The brothers (eager) awaited the results.
10. Steve looked (dreamy) out the window.

# Adverbs

## Comparative Adverbs

Adverbs take special forms when they:
- Compare two actions
  - add **-er**, or
  - add **more** if the adverb ends in *-ly* or is more than one syllable
- Compare three or more actions
  - add **-est**, or
  - add **most** if the adverb ends in *-ly*

| Adverb One action | Comparing 2 actions | Comparing 3 or more actions |
|---|---|---|
| Mary ran fast. | Mary ran faster than James. | Elena is the fastest runner of all. |
| Bill works slowly. | Susan works more slowly than Bill. | Albert works most slowly of all. |

Comparative Adverbs, Exercise 1. Complete the chart.

| Adverb | 2 actions | 3 or more actions |
|---|---|---|
| 1. late | later | latest |
| 2. quickly | | |
| 3. quietly | | |
| 4. near | | |
| 5. recently | | |
| 6. deep | | |
| 7. far | | |
| 8. eagerly | | |
| 9. soon | | |
| 10. playfully | | |
| 11. freely | | |
| 12. closely | | |

Comparative Adverbs, Exercise 2.  Write the correct form for each adverb in parentheses.  Not all forms need changing.

1. The rain fell (hard) than during the last storm.
2. Paul arrived (early) of all students.
3. We talked (softly) than we did before.
4. Each can be done (easily) than the next.
5. The captain walked (quickly) than the rest of the team.
6. Of all leaders, she performed (faithfully).
7. He did the chores (easily).
8. Emily finished (soon) than anyone else.
9. Of all people, he can do the job (skillfully).
10. The wind blew (strong) than yesterday.

Comparative Adverbs, Exercise 3.  Underline the correct adverb form.

1. The wind blew (more often  ,  most often) today.
2. Rose worked (harder  ,  hardest) of all.
3. He stood (closer  ,  more close) to the elephant than anyone else.
4. Warren paints (most quickly  ,  more quickly) of all.
5. The tuba has a (lower  ,  more lower) sound than the flute.
6. Cal held the rope (more firmly  ,  more firmer) than Tom.
7. Which sound can you hear (more clearly  ,  most clearly) of all?
8. They sat (more patiently  ,  most patiently) than before.
9. Which of those two cars goes (farther  ,  fartherest)?
10. Who acted (most politely  ,  more politely), John, Marie, or Ted?

# **A**dverbs

## Good - Well and Bad - Badly

---

*Good* and *bad* are adjectives that describe nouns or pronouns.
*Well* and *badly* are adverbs that describe verbs.

---

These four words are often confused.

*Good* and *bad* are adjectives that only describe nouns or pronouns and tell *what kind* . They never describe verbs or adverbs.

| | |
|---|---|
| He was a good friend. | *good* describes the noun *friend.* |
| That was bad news. | *bad* describes the noun *news.* |

*Well* and *badly* are adverbs that only describe verbs and tell *how*. They never describe nouns or pronouns.

| | |
|---|---|
| We lost badly in the finals. | *badly* describes the verb *lost .* |
| Are your plans going well? | *well* describes the verb *going.* |

When *good* , *bad* , *well* , and *badly* are used in comparison, they take these forms:

| Adjective | Comparing 2 nouns or pronouns | Comparing 3 or more nouns or pronouns |
|---|---|---|
| good | better | best |
| bad | worse | worst |

| Adverbs | Comparing 2 verbs | Comparing 3 or more nouns or pronouns |
|---|---|---|
| well | better | best |
| badly | worse | worst |

Notice that *good-well* and *bad-badly* have the same comparative forms.

Good/Well and Bad/Badly, Exercise 1. Decide if the word underlined is a noun or verb. Circle the correct word in parentheses.

1. My father <u>taught</u> me _____ . (good , well)
2. He <u>behaved</u> _____ . (bad , badly)
3. I wish I <u>could run</u> as _____ as George. (good , well)
4. Megan and I had a _____ <u>fight</u>. (bad , badly)
5. Our meeting <u>went</u> _____ . (well , good)
6. My friend and I had a _____ <u>quarrel</u>. (bad , badly)
7. He ate a _____ <u>lunch</u>. (good , well)
8. She <u>performed</u> the dance _____ . (bad , badly)
9. Your family <u>picture</u> is very _____ . (good , well)
10. Our friends <u>needed</u> help _____ . (bad , badly)
11. He gave _____ <u>answers</u> to the questions. (good , well)
12. He <u>answered</u> the questions _____ . (good , well)
13. She did a _____ <u>job</u> on the assignment. (good , well)
14. I think that is a _____ <u>idea</u>. (bad , badly)
15. Our relatives always <u>treat</u> us _____ . (good , well)

Good/Well and Bad/Badly, Exercise 2. Use the correct comparative form for the word in parentheses.

1. Last year was the _____ year for all of us. (good)
2. He played his _____ game ever. (bad)
3. She felt _____ today than yesterday. (well)
4. Of all the piano students, he performed _____ . (badly)
5. We have a _____ team this year. (bad)

Good/Well and Bad/Badly, Exercise 3. Underline all adjectives and adverbs. Place an **n** over nouns or **v** over the verbs they describe.

1. I paint small objects best.
2. We had good weather during our recent vacation.
3. Ruth sings well by herself.
4. We badly needed a new carpet.
5. A good instructor explains everything.

# Review

A. Underline all adverbs in each sentence.
1. She walked very slowly home.
2. We began work early each morning.
3. Our family often visits the beach.
4. They ran around and quietly left.
5. I politely introduced myself and carefully checked the door.
6. Today my parents unexpectedly received an answer.
7. The bird flew swiftly away.
8. The pilot said to fasten our seat belts securely.
9. The audience clapped wildly.
10. Yesterday Jane suddenly finished her work.

B. Tell whether the underlined adverb describes a verb, an adjective, or another adverb.
1. The dog moved <u>quickly</u>.
2. The package will arrive <u>tomorrow</u>.
3. I forget my lunch <u>too</u> often.
4. The movie was <u>extremely</u> long.
5. The animals were <u>very</u> quiet.

C. Underline the correct comparative form in the parentheses.
1. They worked (steadily , most steadily) for an hour.
2. Bring the clothes (quick , quickly).
3. Our team finished (earliest , earlier) of all.
4. Ellen works (more carefully , most carefully) than you do.
5. I can jump (higher , more higher) than you can.

D. Give the correct comparative form of the word in parentheses.
1. The boys walked (slowly) than the girls.
2. Who worked (hard) of all?
3. Is your house (near) to the store than mine?
4. We should dress (warmly) in the winter than in the summer.
5. Our class watched (excitedly) of all.

# Final Assessment Test

## Adjectives

A. Underline all adjectives including articles.
1. The Catholic church is across the street from the Jewish synagogue.
2. Three red cars lead the entire parade.
3. She ran quickly home without stopping.
4. This one is mine.
5. They bought a beautiful home on a quiet street.

B. Underline the correct adjective.
1. (A , An) entire week passed before he came.
2. (A , An) large elephant walked around (this , those) houses.
3. The cat left through (a , an) open window (this , those) morning.
4. Take (this , these) books home with you.
5. (This , Those) doctors are very polite.

C. Add the comparative adjectives for the words given.

| Adjective | Comparing 2 | Comparing 3 or more |
| --- | --- | --- |
| 1. fast | | |
| 2. exciting | | |
| 3. near | | |
| 4. expensive | | |
| 5. beautiful | | |
| 6. young | | |
| 7. bad | | |
| 8. good | | |
| 9. active | | |
| 10. messy | | |

## Adverbs

A. Underline each adverb.
1. She put away her new clothes.
2. We recently visited Europe.
3. The group arrived too soon.
4. I would rather go now.
5. What time will they come here?

6. The large crowd was very quiet.
7. The motor boat arrived yesterday.
8. They quickly opened their beautiful presents.
9. The big dog walked clumsily on the wet floor.
10. She jumped easily over the limb.

B Make an adverb from these adjectives.

| | | | |
|---|---|---|---|
| 1. merry | 3. low | 5. quiet | 7. sharp |
| 2. fair | 4. real | 6. humble | 8. meek |

C. Write a correct comparative form, if needed, for the adjectives in parentheses.
1. Ellen worked (quickly) than her friend.
2. John left (late) than he did yesterday.
3. He can do the job (skillfully) of all.
4. The herd moved (slowly).
5. Emily was the (fast) runner of all.

D. Underline the correct word in each sentence.
1. I wish I could run as (well , good) as you.
2. We lost (bad , badly) at the game.
3. I feel (better , best) today than yesterday.
4. Which of these two is (worse , worst)?
5. Which one is the (worse , worst) answer of all?

# ANSWERS

## Beginning Assessment Test, Page 1.

### Part 1: Adjectives

A. Underline all adjectives.
1. <u>Twelve</u> people came to <u>this</u> party.
2. We have <u>few</u> friends in <u>that</u> state.
3. <u>French</u>, <u>African</u>, and <u>Asian</u> nationalities were present.
4. <u>Our Persian</u> cat is <u>black</u> and <u>white</u>.
5. They drove <u>many</u> hours and <u>long</u> distances to get home.

B. Circle the correct pronoun in parentheses.
1. (The), A) two brothers went to (an , (a)) movie.
2. ((This), These) was (a , (an)) honest mistake.
3. How many people bought (this , (those)) shoes?
4. (The), An) car went ((this) , these) way.
5. The cat left through (a , (an)) open window ((this) , those) morning.

C. Comparative adjectives.  Write the missing form for each adjective.

| Adjective | comparing 2 | comparing 3 or more |
|---|---|---|
| 1. pretty | prettier | **prettiest** |
| 2. tall | **taller** | tallest |
| 3. difficult | more difficult | **most difficult** |
| 4. joyful | **more joyful** | most joyful |
| 5. good | **better** | **best** |
| 6. exciting | **more exciting** | most exciting |
| 7. near | **nearer** | nearest |
| 8. bad | **worse** | **worst** |
| 9. small | **smaller** | **smallest** |
| 10. active | **more active** | **most active** |

### Part 2: Adverbs

A. Underline all adverbs.
1. We <u>always</u> go home.
2. They have an <u>extremely</u> large house.
3. We <u>finally</u> found the ball.
4. She <u>completely</u> built the model.
5. They are <u>very</u> popular brothers.
6. They lived <u>there</u> for <u>almost</u> five years.
7. The car moved <u>quickly</u> down the street.

B. Make an adverb from these adjectives.
1. slow- **slowly**      3. gentle- **gently**      5. busy- **busily**
2. careful- **carefully**   4. noisy- **noisily**      6. careless- **carelessly**

C. Write the correct comparative form of each adjective in parentheses.
    1. John studied **hardest** of all.
    2. We left **later** than yesterday.
    3. She answered **more quickly** than Albert.
    4. Susan worked **most carefully** of all.
    5. I will arrive **sooner** than you.

D. Good-bad/well-badly. Underline the correct word in each sentence.
    1. I wish I could run as (<u>well</u> , good) as you.
    2. We lost (bad , <u>badly</u>) at the game.
    3. I felt (<u>better</u> , best) today than yesterday.
    4. He played his (badest , <u>worst</u>) game ever.
    5. Which is the (worse , <u>worst</u>) answer of all?

**Adjectives, Exercise 1.  Page 3.**
    Answers will vary.

**Adjectives, Exercise 2.  Page 4.**
    1. big = what kind; green = what kind
    2. That = which one; twenty = how many
    3. Both = which one; expensive = what kind
    4. This = which one; young = what kind; twice = how many
    5. silly = what kind
    6. These = which one; wet = what kind; slippery = what kind
    7. hungry = what kind
    8. purple, red = what kind; favorite = what kind; two = how many
    9. that = which one; valuable = what kind
    10. several = how many; food = what kind

**Adjectives, Exercise 3.  Page 4.**
    Answers will vary.

**Adjectives, Exercise 4.  Page 4.**
    1. The (soccer) players wore (red) shirts.
    2. (Each) player was from a (different) town.
    3. They were (state) champions for (three) years.
    4. They are (funny) to watch.
    5. (One) player will tell a (funny) joke.
    6. I understand why they like (that) sport.
    7. (That) player lives in a (small) town which has (two) names.
    8. (Practice) games are (every) Tuesday at a (community) center.
    9. The (next) (home) game is (four) (long) weeks away.
    10. That will give us (enough) time to buy (good) tickets.

**Adjectives, Exercise 5. Page 4**
    1. Winter = what kind; six = how many
    2. clear, white, beautiful = what kind
    3. late, early = what kind
    4. Young = what kind; last = which one
    5. Those = which one; strong = what kind; many = how many
    6. Some = how many; wild = what kind
    7. bright = what kind; growing = what kind
    8. golden = what kind; wild = what kind
    9. Warm = what kind; few = how many
    10. Those = which one; another = which one

**Adjectives, Exercise 6.  Page 5.**
　　　Answers will vary.

**Proper Adjectives, Exercise 1.  Page 6.**
　　　1. American
　　　2. Swedish
　　　3. Spanish
　　　4. Alaskan
　　　5. North American
　　　6. Mexican
　　　7. Indian
　　　8. Chinese
　　　9. Polish
　　　10. French.

**Proper Adjectives, Exercise 2.  Page 6.**
　　　1. Roman statues
　　　2. Canadian bacon
　　　3. Hawaiian pineapples
　　　4. Arabian stories
　　　5. French bread
　　　6. Florida juice
　　　7. Italian pizza
　　　8. Sandinavian furniture
　　　9. Scottish wool
　　　10. Southern folk songs

**Articles, Exercise 1.  Page 7.**
　　　1. The two brothers went to a movie.
　　　2. Can you wash the plates?
　　　3. An unusual cat ran to the door.
　　　4. I received a card from an old uncle in Virginia.
　　　5. We will go home after the play.
　　　6. Let's take the picture home.
　　　7. We took a walk across town.
　　　8. How far away is the school you attend?
　　　9. We took a boat to an island.
　　　10. He ran around the track twice.

**Articles, Exercise 2.  Page 7.**
　　　1. A
　　　2. a
　　　3. A
　　　4. an
　　　5. a
　　　6. The
　　　7. an
　　　8. a, a
　　　9. The, the
　　　10. a

**Demonstrative Adjectives, Exercise 1. Page 8.**
　　　1. This book is about famous inventors.
　　　2. How many people bought those shoes?
　　　3. That doctor is very polite.
　　　4. Please hand me those papers.
　　　5. They were not going to that house.
　　　6. Take these books home with you.
　　　7. Take that box of wood.
　　　8. Those old stories are enjoyable.
　　　9. That green glass has a crack.
　　　10. Many strange insects are found in these Western states.

28

**Demonstrative Adjectives, Exercise 2. Page 9.**
1. **This** hat belongs to me. **Adjective**
2. **That** is my hat. **Pronoun**
3. **These** books are for you. **Adjective**
4. **These** are for you and your brother. **Pronoun**
5. **Those** go with the shirt. **Pronoun**
6. **This** is your coat. **Pronoun**
7. She took **those** with her. **Pronoun**
8. **Those** shirts must be washed. **Adjective**
9. His cat is **this** one. **Adjective**
10. Give **these** to him. **Pronoun**
11. What is **this**? **Pronoun**
12. **These** are greener. **Pronoun**
13. **That** was fast. **Pronoun**
14. **This** cake is mine. **Adjective**
15. **That** cake is yours. **Adjective**

**Comparative Adjectrives, Exercise 1.  Page 10.**

| Adjective | Two | Three or More |
|---|---|---|
| fast | **faster** | fastest |
| tall | taller | **tallest** |
| popular | **more popular** | most popular |
| **heavy** | heavier | **heaviest** |
| **famous** | more famous | most famous |
| green | **greener** | greenest |
| messy | **messier** | messiest |
| expensive | more expensive | **most expensive** |
| wet | wetter | **wettest** |
| **difficult** | more difficult | **most difficult** |
| pretty | **prettier** | prettiest |
| powerful | **more powerful** | **most powerful** |
| exciting | **more exciting** | **most exciting** |
| beautiful | **more beautiful** | **most beautiful** |
| active | **more active** | **most active** |
| small | **smaller** | **smallest** |
| young | **younger** | **youngest** |
| successful | **more successful** | **most successful** |
| hot | **hotter** | **hottest** |
| new | **newer** | **newest** |
| wise | **wiser** | **wisest** |
| comfortable | **more comfortable** | **most comfortable** |
| happy | **happier** | **happiest** |
| clever | **more clever** | **most clever** |
| heavy | **heavier** | **heaviest** |

**Comparative Adjectives,  Exercise 2. Page 11.**
1. deepest
2. fastest
3. funniest
4. more difficult
5. prettier
6. most surprising
7. most comfortable
8. nicest
9. warmer
10. flatter

**Comparative Adjectives,  Exercise 3.  Page 11.**
1. most
2. heavier
3. greenest
4. longest
5. harder
6. most beautiful
7. more comfortable
8. freshest
9. fancier
10. light

**Good and Bad, Exercise 1. Page 12.**

| | |
|---|---|
| 1. best | 6. better |
| 2. worse | 7. best |
| 3. best | 8. worst |
| 4. good, better | 9. better |
| 5. worst | 10. bad, worse |

**Good and Bad, Exercise 2. Page 12.**

| | |
|---|---|
| 1. bad | 6. good |
| 2. better | 7. best |
| 3. best | 8. worst |
| 4. worst | 9. worse |
| 5. better | 10. better |

## Review. Page 13.

A. Circle all proper adjectives. Underline all adjectives that tell *what kind* , *how many* , or *which one* .

1. How <u>many</u> people live in the <u>green</u> building?
2. The <u>apple</u> pie was <u>warm</u> and <u>tasty</u>.
3. They are (Washington) apples.
4. <u>Our</u> (Persian) cat is <u>old</u>, but she is <u>beautiful</u>.
5. <u>Wood</u> stoves should burn <u>dry</u> wood.
6. <u>Those</u> <u>tin</u> cans came from the <u>corner</u> market.
7. <u>Some</u> people will bring <u>large</u> boxes.
8. The <u>entire</u> school will attend the <u>free</u> concert.
9. Today is a <u>perfect</u> day to repair the <u>broken</u> door.
10. The <u>last</u> train left <u>ten</u> minutes ago.

B. Underline the correct article or demonstrative adjective.

1. (<u>This</u> , Those) dog is (<u>a</u> , an) golden retriever.
2. (<u>A</u> , An) history test will be given on Friday.
3. Would you rather have a cherry or (a , <u>an</u>) olive?
4. (These , <u>That</u>) book belongs on the top shelf.
5. The work will take (a , <u>an</u>) hour to complete.

C. Use the correct form of the adjective in parentheses.

1. My mother makes the **best** cookies in the world.
2. This is the **worst** storm this year.
3. What is the **longest** day of the year?
4. Is this one or that one **more beautiful** ?
5. The **hardest** part of all is remembering to come on time.
6. That is the **better** recipe of the two.
7. The oak has **stronger** and **heavier** wood than the pine.
8. Your answer is **worse** than his.
9. Which of you two has studied **longer** ?
10. Who is the **most successful** student in your class?

**Adverbs and Verbs, Exercise 1. Page 14.**
1. carefully
2. quietly
3. after
4. here
5. yesterday

**Adverbs and Verbs, Exercise 2. Page 14.**
1. everywhere, carefully
2. Instantly, Suddenly
3. often, happily, now, sometimes
4. early, noisily
5. soon, shortly, loudly

**Adverbs and Verbs, Exercise 3. Page 15.**
1. hungrily =how
2. tonight = when
3. everywhere = where
4. easily = how
5. Nearby = where
6. early = when
7. carefully = how
8. soon = when
9. quietly = how
10. overhead =where

**Adverbs and Verbs, Exercise 4. Page 15.**
1. walked slowly- how
2. dried overnight- when
3. stood above - where
4. won fairly- how
5. was placed inside- where
6. opcned excitedly -how
7. Happily watched - how
8. give sometime - when
9. can jump easily - how
10. Today brought - when

**Adverbs and Verbs, Exercise 5. Page 15.**
Answers will vary.

**Adverbs and Adjectives, Exercise 1. Page 16.**
1. awfully
2. very
3. quite
4. really
5. often
6. extremely
7. unusually
8. very
9. nearly
10. very

**Adverbs and Adjectives, Exercise 2. Page 16.**
Answers will vary.

**Adverbs and Adverbs, Exercise 1. Page 17.**
1. very
2. closely
3. quite
4. too
5. really
6. so
7. very
8. too
9. rather
10. somewhat

**-ly, Exercise 1. Page 18.**
1. quietly
2. quickly
3. suddenly
4. closely
5. surely
6. angrily
7. truthfully
8. happily
9. usually
10. lazily
11. playfully
12. dearly
13. simply
14. selfishly
15. sleepily
16. easily
17. carelessly
18. noisily
19. tenderly
20. busily

**-ly, Exercise 2. Page 18.**
1. immediately
2. softly; closely
3. barely
4. terribly
5. possibly
6. extremely; quickly
7. really
8. Sadly; exactly
9. eagerly
10. dreamily

31

## Comparative Adverbs, Exercise 1. Page 19

| Adverb | 2 actions | 3 or more actions |
| --- | --- | --- |
| 1. late | later | latest |
| 2. quickly | **more quickly** | **most quickly** |
| 3. quietly | **more quietly** | **most quietly** |
| 4. near | **nearer** | **nearest** |
| 5. recently | **more recently** | **most recently** |
| 6. deep | **deeper** | **deepest** |
| 7. far | **farther, further** | **farthest, furthest** |
| 8. eagerly | **more eagerly** | **most eagerly** |
| 9. soon | **sooner** | **soonest** |
| 10. playfully | **more playfully** | **most playfully** |
| 11. freely | **more freely** | **most freely** |
| 12. closely | **more closely** | **most closely** |

## Comparative Adverbs, Exercise 2.  Page 20.

1. harder
2. earliest
3. more softly
4. more easily
5. more quickly
6. most faithfully
7. easily
8. sooner
9. most skillfully
10. stronger

## Comparative Adverbs, Exercise 3. Page 20.

1. more often
2. hardest
3. closer
4. most quickly
5. lower
6. more firmly
7. most clearly
8. more patiently
9. faster
10. most politely

## Good/Bad and Well/Badly, Exercise 1. Page 22.

1. well
2. badly
3. well
4. bad
5. well
6. bad
7. good
8. badly
9. good
10. badly
11. good
12. well
13. good
14. bad
15. well

## Good/Bad and Well/Badly, Exercise 2. Page 22.

1. best
2. worst
3. better
4. worst
5. worse

## Good/Bad and Well/Badly, Exercise 3. Page 22.

1. I paint small objects best.
2. We had good weather during our recent vacation.
3. Ruth sings well by herself.
4. We badly needed a new carpet.
5. A good instructor explains everything.

## Review.  Page 23

A. Underline any adverbs in each sentence.

1. She walked very slowly home.
2. We began work early each morning.
3. Our family often visits the beach.
4. They ran around and quietly left.

5. I <u>politely</u> introduced myself and <u>carefully</u> checked the door.
6. <u>Today</u> my parents <u>unexpectedly</u> received an answer.
7. The bird flew <u>swiftly</u> away.
8. The pilot said to fasten our seat belts <u>securely</u>.
9. The audience clapped <u>wildly</u>.
10. <u>Yesterday</u> Jane <u>suddenly</u> finished her work.

B. Tell whether the underlined adverb describes a verb, an adjective, or another adverb.
1. The dog moved <u>quickly</u>. **verb**
2. The package will arrive <u>tomorrow</u>. **verb**
3. I forget my lunch <u>too</u> often. **adverb**
4. The movie was <u>extremely</u> long. **adjective**
5. The animals were <u>very</u> quiet. **adjective**

C. Underline the correct comparative form in the parentheses.
1. They worked (<u>steadily</u> , most steadily) for an hour.
2. Bring the clothes (quick , <u>quickly</u>).
3. Our team finished (<u>earliest</u> , earlier) of all.
4. Ellen works (<u>more carefully</u> , most carefully) than you do.
5. I can jump (<u>higher</u> , more higher) than you can.

D. Give the correct comparative form of the word in parentheses.
1. The boys walked **more slowly** than the girls.
2. Who worked **hardest** of all?
3. Is your house **nearer** to the store than mine?
4. We should dress **more warmly** in the winter than in the summer.
5. Our class watched **most excitedly** of all.

# Final Assessment Test.  Page 24

## Adjectives
A. Underline all adjectives including articles.
1. <u>The</u> <u>Catholic</u> church is across <u>the</u> street from <u>the</u> <u>Jewish</u> synagogue.
2. <u>Three</u> <u>red</u> cars lead <u>the</u> <u>entire</u> parade.
3. She ran quickly home without stopping.
4. <u>This</u> one is mine.
5. They bought <u>a</u> <u>beautiful</u> home on <u>a</u> <u>quiet</u> street.

B. Underline the correct adjective.
1. (A , <u>An</u>) entire week passed before he came.
2. (<u>A</u> , An) large elephant walked around (this , <u>those</u>) houses.
3. The cat left through (a , <u>an</u>) open window (<u>this</u> , those) morning.
4. Take (this , <u>these</u>) books home with you.
5. (This , <u>Those</u>) doctors are very polite.

C. Add the comparative adjectives for the words given.

| 1. fast | **faster** | **fastest** |
|---|---|---|
| 2. exciting | **more exciting** | **most exciting** |
| 3. near | **nearer** | **nearest** |
| 4. expensive | **more expensive** | **most expensive** |
| 5. beautiful | **more beautiful** | **most beautiful** |
| 6. young | **younger** | **youngest** |
| 7. bad | **worse** | **worst** |
| 8. good | **better** | **best** |

| 9. active | **more active** | **most active** |
|-----------|----------------|-----------------|
| 10. messy | **messier** | **messiest** |

## Adverbs

A. Underline each adverb.
1. She put <u>away</u> her new clothes.
2. We <u>recently</u> visited Europe.
3. The group arrived <u>too</u> <u>soon</u>.
4. I would <u>rather</u> go <u>now</u>.
5. What time will they come <u>here</u>?
6. The large crowd was <u>very</u> quiet.
7. The motor boat arrived <u>yesterday</u>.
8. They <u>quickly</u> opened their beautiful presents.
9. The big dog walked <u>clumsily</u> on the wet floor.
10. She jumped <u>easily</u> over the limb.

B Make an adverb from these adjectives.
1. merry = **merrily**    3. low = **lowly**    5. quiet = **quietly**    7. sharp = **sharply**
2. fair = **fairly**    4. real = **really**    6. humble = **humbly**    8. meek = **meekly**

C. Write a correct comparative form, if needed, for the adjectives in parentheses.
1. Ellen worked **more quickly** than her friend.
2. John left **later** than he did yesterday.
3. He can do the job **most skillfully** of all.
4. The herd moved **more slowly**.
5. Emily was the **fastest** runner of all.

D. Underline the correct word in each sentence.
1. I wish I could run as (<u>well</u> , good) as you.
2. We lost (bad , <u>badly</u>) at the game.
3. I feel (<u>better</u> , best) today than yesterday.
4. Which of these two is (<u>worse</u> , worst)?
5. Which one is the (worse , <u>worst</u>) answer of all?